A Leaf Can Be...

by Laura Purdie Salas

illustrations by Violeta Dabija

M MILLBROOK PRESS · MINNEAPOLIS

For Maddie, who can be all the
wonder of the world —L.P.S.

To my dad, who taught me to
draw and love it —V.D.

Millbrook Press
A division of Lerner Publishing Group, Inc.
241 First Avenue North
Minneapolis, MN 55401 USA

Website address: www.lernerbooks.com

Main body text set in GFY Brutus 28/42.
Typeface provided by The Chank Company.

Library of Congress Cataloging-in-Publication Data

Salas, Laura Purdie.
  A leaf can be— / by Laura Purdie Salas ; illustrations by Violeta Dabija.
    p.   cm.
  Summary: Rhyming text and illustrations explore some of the many things a
leaf can be, from tree topper to rain stopper. Includes facts about leaves and
a glossary.
  ISBN: 978-0-7613-6203-6 (lib. bdg. : alk. paper)
  [1. Stories in rhyme. 2. Leaves—Fiction.] I. Dabija, Violeta, ill. II. Title.
PZ8.3.S166Le 2012
[E]—dc23   2011022227

Manufactured in the United States of America
1 – CG – 12/31/11

A leaf is a leaf.
It bursts out each spring
when sunny days linger
and orioles sing.

A leaf can be a...

Soft cradle

Water ladle

Sun taker

Food maker

Tree topper

Rain stopper

Skin welter

Air cleaner

Mouth filler

Shade spiller

Bat shelter

Earth greener

A leaf is a leaf—
a bit of a tree.
But when cool days come chasing,
it also can be a...

Wind rider

Lake glider

Pile grower

Hill glow-er

Frost catcher

Moth matcher

Fine healer

Snake concealer

Ground warmer

Nest former

A leaf is a leaf—
a bit of a tree.
Now go and discover
what else it can be!

More about Leaves

We all know leaves grow on trees and other plants. But did you know that leaves have many jobs? Some are practical, like making food for the tree. Others are beautiful or fun, like dancing in the wind.

Soft cradle: Certain kinds of caterpillars spin cocoons around themselves and turn into moths. Some caterpillars spin their cocoon right on leaves. The leaf acts as a cradle, keeping the cocoon safe until the moth comes out.

Water ladle: Animals don't use bowls or spoons or cups. But many drink out of leaves! Leaves' shape makes them perfect for holding dew or rainwater.

Sun taker: One of the major jobs of a leaf is to take in sunlight.

Food maker: Along with the sunlight, leaves take in air and water. They turn these things into food for the plant or the tree. This is called photosynthesis.

Tree topper: This is how we usually think of leaves: the green tops of trees. Imagine what the world would look like if trees were only trunks and limbs, with no leaves.

Rain stopper: Flat, broad leaves shelter things underneath the tree from rain. Never stand under a tree during a thunderstorm, though!

Skin welter: Not all leaves are nice to touch. Poison ivy will cause red, itchy bumps—or welts—to form on skin.

Bat shelter: Some leaves shelter animals. Tiny Honduran white bats, for instance, make a line down the center of a large, rain forest leaf. They chew through some of the leaf's veins, and the leaf folds down around them like a tent.

Shade spiller: On a hot, August day, what could be better than the cool shade of an oak tree?

Mouth filler: Leaves can be tasty! Apes, giraffes, insects, and many other animals eat leaves. Humans do too. Have you eaten lettuce or spinach lately?

Air cleaner: When leaves take in air, they also take tiny bits of pollution out of the air. Leaves also send out clean oxygen, a chemical in the air that people need to breathe.

Earth greener: Things that keep land, water, and air healthy are called green. Leaves, plants, and trees are called green not only because of their color but also because they do good things for our planet.

Wind rider: When leaves die and fall off a tree, they swirl in the wind. Watch the blowing leaves and you'll see which way the wind is going.

Lake glider: Some leaves skim across the surface of a lake like tiny sailboats.

Pile grower: Raking the yard might be a chore, but jumping in a big pile of leaves makes it all worthwhile!

Hill glow-er: In fall, the weather cools off and days grow shorter. Leaves stop making chlorophyll, the substance that turns them green. Then we can see the gold, orange, and red colors of some leaves.

Frost catcher: When the air gets cold overnight, frost sometimes forms on leaves. It turns them white and sparkly.

Moth matcher: Some moths and other animals look like leaves. This helps the animals blend in with their surroundings and hide from other animals that would eat them. Dead-leaf moths look like, well . . . dead, brown, autumn leaves.

Fine healer: Some plants can be used as ingredients in medicines.

Snake concealer: Snakes sometimes slither under a layer of leaves lying on the ground. The leaves hide the snakes from hawks, rats, and other hungry animals.

Ground warmer: When fallen leaves cover the ground each autumn, they have a job to do. They help warm the ground below them for the winter. That helps the grass underneath survive until spring.

Nest former: Many birds use dried leaves from the autumn before to build their nests each spring.

Glossary

chlorophyll: a substance in leaves that makes them green

cocoons: silky coverings certain caterpillars form around themselves before turning into moths

concealer: something that hides something else

frost: tiny bits of ice

ladle: a deep, long spoon to serve soup with

linger: stay awhile

orioles: a kind of bird

photosynthesis: the way leaves use sunlight, air, and water to make food for plants

pollution: things that make the air, land, or water dirty

shelter: home or a safe place to stay

survive: stay alive

veins: tiny tubes in leaves

welts: raised, red lumps on the skin

Further Reading

Lunis, Natalie. *Katydids: Leaf Look-Alikes*. New York: Bearport, 2010.

Rustad, Martha E. H. *Fall Leaves: Colorful and Crunchy*. Minneapolis: Millbrook Press, 2012.

Sterling, Kristin. *Exploring Leaves*. Minneapolis: Lerner Publications Company, 2012.

Wallace, Nancy Elizabeth. *Leaves! Leaves! Leaves!* Tarrytown, NY: Marshall Cavendish, 2003.